Basic English Grammar for New and Prospective ESL Teachers

D1630944

CELTA Preparation

By Miles Jaworski

Other books by this author

102 ESL Games and Activities for New and Prospective Teachers

102 ESL Games and Activities for Kids

English Grammar Exercises: A Complete Guide to English Tenses for ESL Students

Table of Contents

Introduction

If you're planning to teach English abroad, let me congratulate you on making an excellent decision. ESL teaching can be very rewarding and is a wonderful way to experience a different culture first-hand. Your time living and working abroad will no doubt make an indelible impression upon you and possibly shape the rest of your life.

It's not all roses though. The first year or so of teaching can be very challenging indeed as you adapt to a new country and a new job. And, if things aren't going well in the classroom, it can be very stressful. When your classes are going well, however, everything else tends to fall into place. Fundamental to giving good quality lessons is a basic knowledge of the concepts and structures that make the English language work. This basic knowledge will enable you to plan lessons quicker and to give quality lessons that both you and your students will enjoy.

This book outlines, illustrates and explains all the essential grammatical structures you will encounter when teaching students from a beginner to intermediate / upper-intermediate level. I strongly recommend that you read this book from cover to cover initially, and that you then use it as a reference throughout your courses.

If you find this book useful and would like to look at ways of teaching some of the grammar you have learned, you may be interested in 102 ESL Games and Activities for New and Prospective Teachers. This book lists fun, interactive ways for your students to practice grammatical structures and vocabulary in the classroom as well as methods to increase their fluency.

The tenses

An understanding of English tenses is vital to understanding how the language works. Very simply put, we use tense in order to place a state or action within a specific time. Let's look at the 12 different English tenses in the approximate order that you are likely to encounter them in the classroom.

The present simple tense

Structure: Subject + present verb

Examples: "Water (subject) boils (present verb) at 100 degrees Celsius" or, "I (subject) drink (present verb) coffee in the morning."

This is the most common of our tenses and makes up something like 80% of our speech – so best to know what it is! The most important thing to remember about this tense, is that we don't really use it to talk about the present! Instead we use it for two primary purposes:

1. To talk about facts or truths. As in our first example above, "Water boils at 100 degrees Celsius." This is a fact. Or as in, "My brother is friendly," "My car is very temperamental" or, "I have lots of dogs."

2. To talk about things that habitually happen (generally I use the word "always" instead of habitual with my

students,) as in our second example above, "I drink coffee in the morning." This is a habit of mine. I do it everyday, or at least most days. Or, "He goes to work at seven in the morning," "Tony runs seven miles every day" and, "He brings his wife breakfast in bed every Saturday."

The present continuous tense

Structure: Subject + present form of the verb "to be" + present participle

Examples: "I (subject) am (to be) running (present participle)" or, "They (subject) are (to be) enjoying (present participle) the movie."

We use this tense for two main reasons:

1. To talk about things that are happening now. For example, "You are reading this text," "The world is turning" or, "The sun is shining." This usage of the present continuous is one that most students grasp very quickly and easily although bringing into class pictures of people performing various actions can aid understanding, e.g., "He is swimming" etc.

2. To talk about future appointments and arrangements. For example, "I'm meeting David at the Pub tonight" or, "I'm picking up my sister from the airport tomorrow." Students tend to find this usage of the present continuous tense more difficult to grasp. You can aid their understanding by explaining that if it is something you might note down on a calendar or in an appointment book

then you would use the present continuous tense.

The past simple tense

Structure: Subject + past verb

Examples: "I (subject) went (past verb) to the bank yesterday" or, "We (subject) went (past verb) on holiday to Greece last year.

We use the past tense in two primary ways:

1. To talk about things that started and finished at a specific time in the past and which have no connection to the present. For example, "I went to the pool yesterday," "I saw a football match last year" or, "I got married in 1993." As you can see from the examples, we often add a time word or phrase to the sentence.

2. To talk about a sequence of events that occurred in the past; a narrative or story. For example, "I got up at six, and then I made a coffee. After that, I walked to the gym and started exercising. Then..," etc. As you can see from the example, we often add sequencing words such as, "first," "then" and, "after that" when using this tense.

The present perfect tense

Structure: Subject + have/has + past participle

Examples: "They (subject) have (have) been (past

participle) to Brazil," "She (subject) has (has) eaten (past participle) breakfast" or, "I (subject) have (have) lived (past participle) in the U.S for six years."

The present perfect tense is a wonderfully versatile tense and is often explained as "the unfinished past." I find this phrase wonderfully vague and ambiguous, however, and prefer to break the tense into its three primary uses:

1. To talk about experiences that occurred *at some time* in the past. Not a specific time, just some time, hence, we can't add date or time words to the sentence. For example, "I have eaten grasshoppers." If we then want to go on and talk more specifically about this experience because, for example, someone wanted more information, we would switch to the past simple tense, e.g., "Yes, it was in Thailand six years ago. They were delicious!"

2. To talk about a past action that has a result in the present. For example, "I've washed the car," (I washed the car in the past and it is NOW clean,) "I've had breakfast," (I ate breakfast in the past and I am now full) or, "It has rained" (It rained in the past and the ground is now wet.)

3. To talk about an action that began in the past and continues into the present (and perhaps into the future.) It is common to use "for" and "since" with this usage of the present perfect in order to indicate how long this action or state has continued for. For example, "I have studied ancient history for six years" or, "I have been overweight since 2008."

The future simple tense

Structure: Subject + will + base form of the verb

Examples: "The Olympic Games (subject) will (will) boost (base form of a verb) the local economy" or, "I (subject) will (will) make (base form of a verb) you a coffee."

The future simple tense is often overused by students who seem to think that when you talk about the future you should always use, "will." This is not so and it is important that you and they are clear on the two primary uses of this tense:

1. To make predictions or assumptions about the future. For example, "The party will be fun," "John will be here at about 10:00" or, "By the year 2076 humans will live on another planet." It's simply what we think will happen. There is no aspect of intention or planning.

2. To express a spontaneous or instant decision. Again no planning is involved. For example if a student has lost her pen you might say, "Here. I'll lend you mine" or if, during a family meal, the door bell goes, someone might say, "I'll get it."

The past continuous tense

Structure: Subject + past form of the verb "to be" + present participle

Example: "They (subject) were (past of "to be") swimming (present participle)" or, "She (subject) was (to be) eating (present participle.)"

We use the past continuous tense in three primary ways:

1. To talk about action that was occurring before and after a specific time in the past. For example, "At 9:00 p.m. yesterday I was getting ready for bed" (Before 9:00 p.m. I was getting ready for bed, at 9:00 p.m. I was getting ready for bed and after 9:00 p.m. I was getting ready for bed.)

2. To set the scene of a narrative or story (a narrative, of course, is primarily told in the past simple tense.) For example, "I was lying in bed, watching TV when the door bell rang" or, "It was raining hard and I was feeling really cold. But then I saw something that cheered me up no end..."

3. To talk about two or more actions occurring at the same time in the past. For example, "While I was getting ready for work, the children were playing" or, "While David was cleaning the car, his son was preparing dinner, and his wife was paying the bills at the bank."

The present perfect continuous tense

Structure: Subject + have/has + been + present participle

Example: "I (subject) have (have) been (been) running

(present participle)" or, "He (subject) has (has) been (been) living (present participle) in France."

Students should begin becoming familiar with this tense from a pre-intermediate level. It emphasizes the continuity of an action or state that takes place over a period of time from the past to the present (and possibly into the future). We use it in two main ways:

1. To talk about an action that began in the past and that has recently finished. As with the present perfect tense, there is often a result aspect to this. For example, imagine your child returning home all wet and muddy. "What have you been doing?" you might ask. And he might reply, "I've been playing in the park." Or, consider getting up in the morning and seeing puddles of water on the ground; "It's been raining," you might exclaim.

2. To talk about an action that began in the past, continues up to the present and may well continue into the future. For example, "I've been working for six hours" (I started work in the past, am still working and probably will into the future) or, "he's been sleeping all day" (he fell asleep last night or in the morning and still hasn't gotten up yet.)

Note: For non-native speakers choosing between the present perfect tense and the present perfect continuous can often be difficult. In most cases we use the simple form to emphasize the result of a past action and the continuous form to emphasize the duration of an action or state. This is why we tend, just tend mind, to use "for" and "since" more often with the continuous form.

We also tend to choose the present perfect simple tense to emphasize permanence and the continuous form to emphasize a possible temporary nature. For example, "I've lived in England for 20 years" (I am in all probability English and have no intention of leaving my home country.) Compare that example to, "I've been living in England for 20 years" (It is likely that I am not English and do not consider it my home.)

The future simple continuous tense

Structure: Subject + will + be + present participle

Examples: "I (subject) will (will) be (be) swimming (present participle) tomorrow afternoon" or, "They (subject) will (will) be (be) doing (present participle) their homework when you get home."

This tense is usually introduced to students at an intermediate level. It presents no particular comprehension problems as long as the students are already familiar with the future simple tense and the present or past continuous tense.

We use the future simple continuous tense in two primary ways:

1. To talk about an action occurring at a specific time in the future. The action will start before the future time and will (probably) continue after this future time. For example, "I'll be watching TV tomorrow at 11:00 p.m." (I will have started watching TV before 11:00 p.m., be

watching TV at 11:00pm and in all likelihood continue watching after 11:00 p.m.) or, "She'll be working through her lunch break tomorrow" (she will start working before her lunch break, continue working through her lunch break and in all probability will not stop when her lunch break is over!)

2. To talk about two or more actions occurring simultaneously at a specific time in the future. For example, "When I get home tomorrow, my brother will be doing his homework, and my sister will be listening to music" or, "Tony will be eating dinner, Mark will be chatting to his girlfriend, and Jane will be listening to music at 9:00 p.m. tomorrow night."

The past perfect tense

Structure: Subject + had + past participle

Examples: "I (subject) had (had) eaten (past participle)" or, "We (subject) had (had) seen (past participle) the movie"

This tense often presents conceptual problems for students. Fortunately, it is not a tense we use overmuch but is very useful when, along with the past continuous, we use the past simple to present a narrative, or story. You can avoid conceptual problems by ensuring that you do not present this tense too early in the students language development and by having a firm grasp of its use yourself. We usually start to introduce this tense during the latter part of a pre-intermediate course and develop fuller comprehension during an intermediate level course.

We use the past perfect tense in two primary ways:

1. To talk about an action that occurred in the past before another action in the past. For this reason we often use it in conjunction with the past simple (for the "other" action in the past.) For example, "I had already eaten dinner but ate the sandwich anyway" or, "She had forgotten her glasses so couldn't watch th movie." Or, we can put the past simple first, "I wasn't happy. I had just seen my dog die."

2. To talk about a state that existed up to a second time/action in the past. Again, this is used in conjunction with past simple. For example, "I'd been lonely for too long and was delighted to meet Ernest" or "When I got to the bar, John had been there for 6 hours."

The past perfect continuous tense

Structure: Subject + had + been + present participle

Examples: "He (subject) had (had) been (been) swimming (present participle)" or "They (subject) had (had) been (been) working (present participle.)"

We generally introduce this structure to students at an upper-intermediate level and use it in one principal way:

1. To talk about an action that began in the past and

continued up to a second time in the past. As with the past perfect tense we commonly use this tense with the past simple tense but unlike the past perfect tense its emphasis is on duration. For example, "I'd been waiting for 6 hours by the time he got there" or "When I finally got my degree I'd been studying for 3 long years." Because of this emphasis on duration it is very often used with time words such as "for" and "since." Often we could use either the past perfect tense or its continuous form, and our choice is often simply one of attitude.

The future perfect simple tense

Structure: Subject + will + have + past participle

Examples: "I (subject) will (will) have (have) finished (past participle) work by the time you arrive" or, "They (subject) will (will) have (have) drunk (past participle) all the wine by the time we get there."

As long as your students have a firm grasp of the present perfect and future simple tenses then this tense should present no particular problems. Generally we would start to introduce this tense to students during an upper-intermediate course.

We use the future perfect tense in two primary ways:

1. To talk about an action in the future that starts and finishes before another action in the future. For example, "Pick me up at about six. I'll have finished my dinner by then" or "He'll have read the book by the time you need

it."

2. To talk about a state that exists up to (and possibly beyond) another time in the future. For example, "I'll have been a student for six years by the time I graduate" or, "We'll have lived in Thailand for six years by then."

The future perfect continuous tense

Structure: Subject + will + have + been + present participle

Examples: "I (subject) will (will) have (have) been (been) traveling (present participle) for 6 hours" or, "They (subject) will (will) have (have) been (been) eating (present participle) lunch for an hour by the time you get there."

We usually introduce this tense to students at a high upper-intermediate or advanced level as its structure is somewhat complex and we use it infrequently. We use this tense in one primary way:

1. To indicate that an action or state will continue up to, and possibly beyond, a specific time in the future. The duration of the action or state is almost invariably mentioned. For example, "We'll have been working since dawn when he brings our lunch" or, "He'll have been living in London for 6 years by the time I visit him."

Direct and indirect objects

In English we use two different types of objects: direct objects and indirect objects. Let's look at the differences between them.

Direct objects

Examples: "I ate a sandwich" or "I saw a pretty girl."

A direct object, answers the question "What?" about the verb. So, as in the examples above, "I ate (what did you eat?) a sandwich" or I saw (what did you see?) a pretty girl," the direct objects are "a sandwich" and "a pretty girl," respectively.

Indirect objects

Examples: "I threw the ball to John" or "We sent him a present."

Remember that indirect objects can't exist without direct objects. So first find the direct object in the sentence by asking "what?" The answers for the examples above are, of course, "the ball" and "a present." Indirect objects answer the question "to whom?" or "For whom?" So, now ask yourself to / for whom for each sentence. So, "I threw the ball to John (to whom?)" and "We sent him a present (to whom?)" As you can clearly see, the indirect object in the first example sentence is, "John" and in the second sentence is "him."

Transitive and intransitive verbs

Transitive verbs take a direct object. Intransitive verbs do not and cannot take a direct object.

Transitive verbs

Structure: Transitive verb + direct object

Examples: "Ariela threw the ball to Gabriel" or "Lisa tells a story to Luca and Clement."

So, in the first example above, we have the transitive verb "threw." We can ask ourselves the question, "What did she throw?" and the answer is, "the ball": the direct object. If we ask ourselves, "to whom / what?" we get the answer, "Gabriel" and this would be the indirect object. In the second example above, we have the transitive verb, "tell." Again, if we ask ourselves the question, "what?" we get the direct object, "a story."

Intransitive verbs

Structure: Intransitive verb (+ compliment, but not direct object.)

Examples: "I laughed at him" or "She cried during the movie."

So, in the first example above, if we ask ourselves the question, "what?" about the verb, it doesn't really make sense: "laughed what?" and so we know the verb is intransitive and does not take a direct object. Sure, other things can follow it, like the prepositional phrase, "at him" but not a direct object. The same applies to the second example above; if we ask ourselves the question, "cried what?" it again makes no sense, and so we can conclude…yes, it is an intransitive verb.

Modal verbs

There are nine modal verbs used in everyday English. These are: can, could, should, must, might, may, would, shall and will. We use modals to express ability, probability, possibility, obligation, expectation, necessity and prohibition, as well as to give advice and permission. The verb following a modal verb is always a base form.

Let's look at all the modals one-by-one.

Can

Structure: Subject + can + base form of the verb

Examples: "I (subject) can (can) swim (base form of the verb)," "You (subject) can (can) go (base form of the verb)" or, "Can (can) I (subject) sit (base form of the verb) down?"

The modal verb, "can" is one of our most used modals and should present very few problems for your students.

We use it in three main ways:

1. To express ability. For example, "She can drive a car," "We can speak Spanish" or, "they can't sing."

2. To give or ask for permission. For example, "You can come in if you want" or, "Can I make myself a cup of tea?"

3. To make requests. For example, "Can I borrow some money?" or, "Can I have another drink please."

Could

Structure: Subject + could + base form of the verb

Examples: "They (subject) could (could) see (base form of the verb) the moon," "Could (could) you (subject) pass (base form of the verb) me the salt?" or, "You (subject) could (could) apply (base form of the verb) for that job."

We use it in three main ways:

1. To express past ability. "I could swim when I was five" or, "She could play the piano when she was 4."

2. To make polite requests. "Could you help me please?" or "Could you pick up the laundry?"

3. To give advice / make suggestions. For example, "You could try harder" or, "You could write a novel!"

Should

Structure: Subject + should + base form of the verb

Examples: "You (subject) should (should) study (base form of the verb) more," "We (subject) should (should) get (base form of the verb) going or we'll be late" or, "I'll ring John. He (subject) should (should) be (base form of the verb) home by now."

We use the modal, "should" in three main ways:

1. To give advice or make recommendations. For example, "You should quit smoking. Its bad for you" or, "You should ask her to marry you!"

2. To express obligation or duty. For example, "You should get to work on time everyday" or, "You should always make time for your children."

3. To express expectation. For example, "It should be easier to get up now that I have a new alarm clock" or, "He should be getting a promotion next year."

Must

Structure: Subject + must + base form of the verb

Examples: "I (subject) must (must) drink (base form of the verb) less coffee," "He (subject) must (must) be (base form of the verb) exhausted" or, "You (subject) must (must) have (base form of the verb) a shave before you go out."

We use the modal, "must" in three main ways:

1. To express personal obligation. We touched on this briefly when looking at "have/ has (got) to." A personal obligation comes from within; it is subjective and not

imposed by others. For example, "I must start going to bed earlier" (I'm fed up with waking up at noon) or, "I must do my laundry today" (All my clothes are dirty and I want to look nice.)

2. To express certainty. For example, "I can't find Mom. She must have gone out" or, "I can hear the phone ringing. That must be Lucy" (We are expecting a phone call from Lucy at this time."

3. To express a strong recommendation. For example, "You must go to that new restaurant on Main Street. The food is amazing!" or, "You must clean your car. It looks terrible."

Might

Structure: Subject + might + base form of the verb

Examples: "It (subject) might (might) rain (base form of the verb) later" or "It (subject) might (might) be (base form of the verb) John."

We use, "might" in two main ways:

1. To express future possibility. For example, "I might visit you later" or "She might buy that coat."

2. To express present possibility. For example, "Mike is really hot. He might be ill" or "We might be late, I'm not sure."

We also use might, very occasionally, to make super polite requests such as, "Might I borrow some money?" or "Might it be ok if I made a cup of coffee?"

May

Structure: Subject + may + base form of the verb

Examples: "I (subject) may (may) be (base form of the verb) putting on weight," "I (subject) may (may) go (base form of the verb) to the movies later" or "May I ask a question?"

We use this modal in three main ways:

1. To express present possibility. For example, "I may be in line for a better job!" or "They may be waiting for us now."

2. To express future possibility. For example, "I may go abroad this summer" or "We may have to stay there overnight."

(Generally speaking, "May" expresses slightly more possibility than "might.")

3. To politely ask for permission to do something. For example, "May I go to John's house?" or "May we watch television?"

Would

Structure: Subject + would + base form of the verb

Examples: "Would (would) you (subject) pass (base form of the verb) me my pen?" "I (subject) would (would) run (base form of the verb) away if a big dog growled at me" or "They said they (subject) would (would) meet (base form of the verb) us there."

The uses of "would" are many. We shall concern ourselves, however, only with the five main uses you are most likely to encounter in classes up to an upper-intermediate level:

1. To make polite requests. For example, "Would you come here a minute, Dave?" or "Would you pick the kids up for me?"

2. To express hypothetical actions or states in the second and third conditionals. For example, "I'd buy a boat! (if I won the lottery!) or "I would have helped you!" (if you had asked.) For more information on the second and third conditionals, please see the conditionals section in this book.

3. To talk about past habits. For example, "When I was a child I would watch television everyday" or "When we were in the Philippines, we'd go swimming all the time."

4. To express future hopes and dreams in conjunction with the word like. For example, "I'd like to be rich one

day" or "I'd like to watch the match tonight."

5. To report speech containing the word "will." For example, "I will go" becomes, "I said I would go" or, "He will eat it" becomes, "She said he would eat it." For more information on reported speech, please see the section in this book.

Shall

Structure: Subject + shall + base form of the verb

Examples: "Shall (shall) we (subject) go (base form of the verb)?" or "Shall (shall) I (subject) put (base form of the verb) the kettle on?"

"Shall" seems to be dying out of everyday English speech somewhat. We do, however, still use it in two main ways:

1. To make suggestions. For example, "Shall we try and fix the bike?" or "Shall we eat now?"

2. To make offers. For example, "Shall I help you?" or "Shall I make dinner?"

Will

Structure: Subject + will + base form of the verb

Examples: "This time next year, Rodney, we (subject) will (will) be (base form of the verb) millionaires!" or "I (subject) will (will) pay (base form of the verb) you next week."

1. To make predictions about the future. For example, "I'll be bald soon!" or "We'll be cold this Christmas."

2. To make promises. For example, "I'll give it back to you tomorrow" or "I'll bring you flowers every day!"

3. To make instant decisions. "It's the phone. I'll answer it" or "You're hungry? I'll make you something."

4. To make offers. For example, "We'll lend you the money if you like." or "C'mon, I'll buy you dinner."

Adverbs of frequency

Structure: adverb of frequency + verb / to be + adverb of frequency

Examples: "I always (adverb of frequency) eat (verb) breakfast in the morning," "They sometimes (adverb of frequency) pick (verb) me up from work" or "I am (to be) seldom (adverb of frequency) unhappy."

We use adverbs of frequency with the present simple tense to talk about how often something happens. "I always brush my teeth in the morning," for example, tells us that this happens 100 percent of the time (approximately.) The normal position for the adverb of frequency is before the verb, but after the verb "to be." For example, "I usually go swimming in the afternoon" but, "She is often late." Let's run through the most common adverbs of frequency with approximate, and I must stress that they are very approximate, percentages. So from the top:
100% of the time: "always"
95% of the time: "almost always"
80% of the time: "usually"
70% of the time: "often"
50% of the time: "sometimes"
35% of the time: "(not) often," for example, "I don't often eat French fries."
20% of the time: "seldom"
10 % of the time: "rarely"
5 % of the time: "hardly ever"
0% of the time: "never"

Possessives

Possessives, of course, tell us who (or what) something belongs to. Let's look at the three major types of possessives: "the possessive 's,'" "possessive adjectives" and "possessive pronouns."

The possessive "s"

Structure: Singular noun + apostrophe "s"

Examples: "That's John's (singular noun + apostrophe "s") book," "That's Clement's (singular noun + apostrophe "s") toy" "That's a nice table. Its leg is a bit bent though."

Fairly simple stuff; with singular nouns we simple add apostrophe "s", so, for example, "John" becomes "John's," "The cat," becomes "The cat's" and so on. As you can see from the third example above, however, there is one exception. This exception is with the word "it." Here we add only the "s", not the apostrophe; so, "Nice dog. I like its waggy tail" or "I didn't like that movie. Its plot was so weak."

Structure: Plural noun + apostrophe ("s")

Examples: "The Jones' new house looks nice." "The tigers' enclosure looks safe" or "The women's section is over there."

Plural nouns generally end in "s" and to these nouns we simply add an apostrophe to show possession, for example, "The brothers' room" or "The rabbits' cage." Some irregular plural nouns don't end in "s" and to these we add apostrophe "s," for example, "The men's room" or "The sheep's field."

Possessive adjectives

Structure: possessive adj + noun

Examples: "It's my (possessive adj) book (noun)," "That is your (possessive adj) room (noun)" or "It's our (possessive adj) mistake (noun.)"

As you can see from the above examples, we place possessive adjectives before a noun.

For "I," the possessive adjective is: "My"
For "You" the possessive adjective is: "Your"
For "He" the possessive adjective is: "His"
For "She" the possessive adjective is: "Her"
For "It" the possessive adjective is: "Its" (no apostrophe)
For "They" the possessive adjective is: "Their"
For "We" the possessive adjective is: "Our"
And for questions, we use "whose," for example, "Whose coat is this?"

Possessive pronouns

Examples: "It's mine (possessive pronoun,)" "Those are his (possessive pronoun)" or "The money is hers

(possessive pronoun.)"

We use possessive pronouns alone, that is, they don't have to come before a noun but refer to a noun (or pronoun) previously mentioned in the sentence.

For "I," the possessive pronoun is: "Mine"
For "You," the possessive pronoun is: "Yours"
For "He," the possessive pronoun is: "His"
For "She," the possessive pronoun is: "Hers"
For "It," the possessive pronoun is: (we don't really have a possessive pronoun for "it." You could use "its" as in, "those are its" but we'd generally avoid this in normal speech.)
For "They," the possessive pronoun is: "Theirs"
For "We," the possessive pronoun is: "Ours"

Some / any

Some and any are quantifiers, that is, they tell us how much / many of something there is. However, these two quantifiers are less than precise! In fact they tell us there is an indefinite amount of something. Nevertheless these two quantifiers are probably the most common of all the quantifiers. Let's look at their different usage:

Some

Structure: some + uncountable/countable noun

Examples: "I've got some (some) money (uncountable noun,)" "They have some (some) good ideas (countable noun)" or "There are some (some) pens (countable noun) over there."

As you can see above, we use, "some" with positive sentences and with both countable and uncountable nouns. (Countable nouns are, as the name suggests, nouns that can be counted like, for example, "books"; we can say "one book," "two books" and so on. Conversely uncountable nouns are, yes you guessed it, nouns that can't be counted, for example, "rice"; we can't say "1 rice" "2 rice" etc.)

Any

Structure: any + uncountable/countable noun

Examples: "I don't have any (any) money (uncountable noun) money," "I haven't got any (any) interest (uncountable noun) in maths" or "Do you have any (any) pets (countable noun)?"

As you can see above, we use "any" with both negative sentences and questions (interrogative sentences) and with both countable and uncountable nouns.

Expressions of quantity

Structure: Expression of quantity + countable / uncountable noun (or noun phrase / noun clause)

Examples: "I've got a few (expression of quantity) books (countable noun) at home," "Have you got many (expression of quantity) things (countable noun) to do?" "I only want a little (expression of quantity) rice (uncountable noun,)" "I've got plenty of (expression of quantity) time (uncountable noun)" or "I've got hardly any (expression of quantity) good ideas (countable noun) for tonight."

Students from a pre-intermediate / intermediate level should be using a variety of expressions of quantity with both countable and uncountable nouns. A countable noun is one that can be counted, for example, "book." You can have "1 book," "2 books," "3 books" and so on, hence, it is countable. Uncountable nouns, of course, can't be counted. Examples include: rice, water, and sugar.

So let's look at some of the more common expressions of frequency.

For countable nouns: "many," "a few," "both," "a couple of," "several," "each," and "every."

For uncountable nouns: "much," "a little," "little," "a bit of," and "a great deal of."

For both: "no," "some," "any," "plenty of," "most," "all,"

"loads of (informal)" and "hardly any."

There are three particular problems that students generally encounter:

1. Students are unsure whether a noun is countable or uncountable or they forget which expressions of quantity are used for which type of noun. Meh, that's part of learning a language. Continued exposure to the language and relevant practice activities should solve this problem.

2. They are unsure of the difference between "a little" and "little" and "a few" and "few." The differences are that: "a little" and "a few" are closer in meaning to "some" and carry no negative meaning; "little" and "few" are closer in meaning to "hardly any," and carry a negative meaning.

3. Students use sentences such as "I have much money" or "She had many dogs." "Much" and "Many" are NOT generally used in spoken English in positive sentences; they are used in negative sentences and questions such as," How many books have you got?" or "I don't have much time."

Yet / still / already

These three adverbs and their varying uses often prove difficult for students to master, especially if they have no equivalent in their native languages. Let's have a look at them in turn.

Yet

Examples: "We haven't finished yet," "It's taking longer than we thought" or "Have you cleaned your room yet?"

We use "yet" in questions and negatives to talk about something we expect to happen or that we expect to have happened. So in the sentence, "We haven't finished yet" the speaker expects to finish at some time in the future. In the sentence, "Have you cleaned your room yet?" the speaker expects the room to already be cleaned or to be cleaned at some time in the future.

In British English, "yet" is usually used with the present perfect tense. In American English it can be used with both the present perfect tense and with the past simple tense. So, "Have you eaten yet?" or "Did you eat yet?"

Still

Examples: "Little Timmy still can't read." or "Are you still in the same job?"

We use "still" to talk about something that has not finished. We often use it when we expected something to be finished earlier. So, "Little Timmy still can't read" (We are really worried about it. He's already 16!) or "Are you still in the same job?" (You always said you hated it. I thought you'd have got a different job by now.)

Unlike, "yet," we use "still" in a variety of different tenses. For example:

The present continuous: "They are still waiting for us to arrive."

The future simple: "I'll still be painting the house next week."

and

The past perfect: "They had still not drunk all the wine when I left."

Already

Examples: "I've already seen this movie," "Have you already eaten?" or "She has already been to most states in America."

We use "already" to talk about something that happened at an earlier time. For example, "I've already seen this movie." We also often use it when something happened at an earlier time than we expected it to. For example, "She has already been to most states in America" (She is only seven) or "I've already made breakfast" (Already? It's only 5:00!)

As with "yet," "still" is commonly used with the present perfect tense in British English, but in both the present perfect and past simple tenses in American English.

Such / so

"Such" and "so" have a very similar meaning to "very." The sentences "Ice is very cold" and "Ice is so cold," for example, carry essentially the same meaning. This concept seems easy to understand for ESL students. It is the differing use of "such" and "so" that often causes problems, even in students of an intermediate level and above. This is strange as the usage is fairly simple and easy to explain.

Such

Structure: Such + adjective + noun / such + noun

Examples: "It's such (such) a beautiful (adjective) day (noun,)" or "You are such (such) a fool (noun.)"

The first example, "It's such a beautiful day," illustrates the most common way we use, "such," that is, with an adjective and a noun. Other examples include, "He's such a funny guy" or "They are such beautiful flowers."

The second example, "You are such a fool" shows a less common, but very interesting way we can use "such," that is, with just a noun to make a judgment about something. Other examples include: "She's such a beauty," "I'm such a catch!" or "It's such idiocy!"

Structure: Such + adjective + noun + that + sentence

Examples: "It was such (such) a hot (adjective) day (noun) that (that) we decided to go to the park (sentence.)" or "She was such (such) a beautiful (adjective) woman (noun) that (that) she became a model (sentence.)"

We can use the structure above to express cause and result. For example, "He was such a careless guy (cause) that he lost all his money (result)" or "They were so tired (cause) that they went straight to bed (result.)"

So

Structure: So + adjective

Examples: "This TV show is so (so) boring (adjective)" or "They are so (so) noisy (noisy.)"

No need to illustrate this structure too much as it is fairly simple; just "so" plus an adjective. Other examples include: "You are so stupid," "Why am I so hungry?" or "English grammar is so interesting!"

Structure: So + adjective + that + sentence

Examples: "I was so (so) angry (angry) that (that) I screamed (sentence)" or "She is so (so) smart (adjective) that (that) she makes me feel stupid (sentence.)"

We can use the structure above to express cause and result. For example, "They were so happy (cause) that they went out to celebrate (result)" or "The movie was so boring (cause) that we left (result.)"

Going to

Structure: Subject + present form of "to be" + going to + base form of the verb

Examples: "I (subject) am (to be) going to (going to) eat (base form of the verb)" or, "It (subject) is (to be) going to (going to) rain (base form of the verb.)"

This structure is extremely important and one that you should be presenting to your students at an elementary level. Often students tend to use, "will" when the, "going to" structure is much more appropriate.

We use this structure in two main ways:

1. To talk about future plans. For example, "I'm going to go to the theater when I'm in Paris" or, "I'm going to make you a nice dinner tonight." Please note that it can be very useful when presenting this structure to contrast it with the future simple tense for instant decisions. This usage of the future simple tense is discussed in the tenses section of this book.

2. To make a future prediction based on present evidence. For example, imagine looking out of your window and seeing dark clouds (the evidence). "It's going to rain (the prediction)" you might say. Or, "This book is so long (the evidence.) It's going to take me ages to finish it."

Used to

Structure: Subject + used to + present verb

Examples: "When I was a teenager I (subject) used to (used to) play (base form of the verb) football every weekend" or "I (subject) didn't use to (used to) read (base form of the verb) much, but now I'm never without a book."

We use this structure in two main ways:

1. To talk about habitual actions in the past which no longer occur now. For example, "She used to drink gin every day" (now she no longer drinks gin every day.) Or alternatively, to talk about habitual actions that didn't occur in the past but now do. For example, "I didn't use to cook a big lunch on Sundays" (Now I do cook a big lunch on Sundays.) Remember, this is for habitual actions that occur again and again, NOT for actions that just occurred once. In that case we would simply use the past simple tense.

2. To talk about states in the past which no longer exist now. For example, "They used to be happy together" (now they are no longer happy together.) Or alternatively, to talk about a state that didn't exist in the past but now does. For example, "He didn't use to have that scar" (now, of course, he does have a scar – perhaps a crocodile!)

There are two things to note about this structure: Firstly,

that if we choose we can replace, "used to" with, "would" when talking about habitual actions. For example, "In the stone age, people used to / would make arrow heads from bits of flint." And secondly, that when used in questions or negatives, the spelling of "used to" changes to, "use to." For example, "Did you use to study hard at school?" or "I didn't use to like just sitting around."

Structure: Subject + to be + used to + present participle

Examples: "I (Subject) am (to be) used to (used to) staying (present participle) up late," "We (subject) are (to be) used to (used to) having (present participle) guests" or, "He (subject) was (to be) used to (used to) getting (present participle) to work late."

We use this structure to say that something is normal and familiar to us; it is not unusual in any way. For example, "People in the west are used to eating three or more times a day." We can use this structure in any non-continuous tense. For example, in the past simple tense "John was used to doing his homework as soon as he got home after school," or in the future simple tense, "He will be used to studying hard after 3 years of college."

Have / has (got) to

Structure: Subject + have / has (+ got) + infinitive verb

Examples: "I (subject) have (have) to cook (infinitive verb) dinner" or, "She (subject) has (has) got (got) to work (infinitive verb) late"

Please note that British English speakers prefer, "have / has got to" while American English speakers prefer, "have / has to."

We use this structure, which makes use of the modal auxiliary verb "have," to talk about an obligation. Specifically an obligation that someone / something impose/s on you, not one you impose on yourself. For example, "I've got to pick up my son at 4:00pm" (The school imposes this obligation as it closes at 4:00pm,) I have to be at work by seven (my boss imposes this obligation and I'll get in trouble if I'm late) or, "I've got to cook dinner" (everybody is hungry and imposing this obligation on me.)

It's a very useful structure which students tend to use far too infrequently, tending to use the less appropriate modal verb, "must" which we tend to use for an obligation we impose upon ourselves. For example, "I must clean my house today" (It's messy and I'd like it to look nice,) "I must quit smoking" (It's bad for me and I'm fed up with coughing all the time) or, "I must lose weight" (I really want to look better.)

The distinction between the two is often hard to grasp and it may help to remind your students simply that "have / has (got) to" is more common when talking about obligation.

The passive voice

Structure: Subject + a form of the verb "to be" + past participle (+ agent)

Examples: "Houses (subject) are (to be) built (past participle) here" or "Human sacrifices (subject) were (to be) made (past participle) by Inca Priests (agent.)"

We use the passive when we wish to focus on the action rather than the agent (doer) of the action. This is usually for one of three primary reasons:

1. We don't know who the agent is. For example, "My house was burgled last night" (by someone, I don't know who.)

2. We don't care who the agent is. For example, "The liquid was boiled to 100 degrees Celsius" (by some scientist; we don't care who.)

3. We don't want to mention the agent. For example, "The oven has been left on all night!" (I don't want to draw attention to the fact that it was I who made this expensive mistake.)

Forming the passive

To form this structure we place what would be the object of an active sentence at the beginning of the sentence to form the subject, insert the verb "to be" in its correct form and change the main verb into a past participle. We do not usually add the "agent," that is, the "doer" of the action to the end of the sentence unless necessary.

Without agent

Active voice: "The I.T specialist has fixed all the computers."

Passive voice: "All the computers have been fixed."

With agent

Active voice: "Electrical faults can cause fire."

Passive voice: "Fire can be caused by electrical faults."

The conditionals

You might also hear these referred to as, "If clauses." We use them, as the name implies, to express condition i.e. if "a" is true then the result is "b." For example, "If I saw a ghost (a), I would scream (b)" or, "If I cut those onions (a), I'll cry (b)."

The most common conditionals are:

The second conditional

Structure: If + past simple tense, subject + would + base form of the verb

Examples: "If (if) I were a dog (past simple tense,) I (subject) would (would) chase (base form of the verb) cats" or, "If (if) I won lots of money (past simple tense,) I (subject) would (would) buy (base form of the verb) a big house."

This conditional tense is a lot of fun to teach, dealing as it does with scenarios that are contrary to fact now, in the present, or dreams and things very unlikely to happen in the future. For example, in the clause, "If I were a dog," we are expressing a scenario that is contrary to fact or unreal now. I am not a dog. But if I were a dog, "I'd chase cats," as this is what dogs do and it looks fun. So, "If I were a dog, I'd chase cats." In the clause, "If I won lots of money," I'm expressing something that is highly unlikely as I only occasionally enter the lottery and the odds against winning are astronomical. But if I did win the lottery, "I'd buy a big house," as it is a dream of mine to live in a big house. So, "If I won the lottery, I'd buy a big house."

The first conditional

Structure: If + present simple tense, future simple tense

Examples: "If (if) you visit us next week (present simple tense,) I'll make a curry (future simple tense)" or, "If (if) they keep drinking (present simple tense,) they will be late for work tomorrow (future simple tense.)"

We use this conditional quite frequently in English to talk about future probabilities or possibilities. For example, in the clause, "If you visit us tomorrow" it is quite possible that you will come to our house tomorrow. Maybe we've talked about it and it is a very possible scenario. And, if you do, "I'll make a curry." I have all the ingredients and I can cook a curry. In the clause, "If they keep drinking," I see it as quite likely they will continue drinking, or a least possible. They are big drinkers, you see, and it won't be the first time they've drunk into the night. If they do, "They'll be late for work," as work starts early and they won't be able to get up in time.

Zero conditional

Structure: If + present simple, present simple

Examples: "If you drink alcohol, you get drunk" or "If a dog bites you, it hurts!"

We use zero conditional for things that are always true. For example, "If you heat water, it boils," "If you eat rotten food, you get sick" or "If you stay out in the sun too long, you get sunburn." These things always happen (well, almost always.) They are facts, or truths.

The third conditional

Structure: If + past perfect, subject + would + present perfect

Examples: "If he had studied harder at University, he would have gotten a better job" or "If she had kissed me, I would have felt so happy!"

We use the third conditional to talk about the past events and results that did not occur and have no possibility of occurring. Both clauses refer to the past and unfortunately we can't change the past.

Commonly we use this structure to express regret. For example, "If we'd eaten breakfast, we wouldn't have spent 15 dollars in that coffee shop," "If you'd taken more care, you wouldn't have crashed my car!" or "If she'd saved her money instead of going out every night, she would have been able to pay her rent."

Or we can use it to express relief. For example, "If we'd been a minute later, we'd have missed the train!" or, "If she hadn't had the brakes checked, we would have died."

Mixed third / second conditional

Structure: If+ past perfect, would + infinitive verb

Examples: "If I'd started learning Italian last year, I'd be fluent by now" or "We'd be able to buy a drink if I hadn't forgotten my wallet."

Here we are looking at events that did or didn't occur in the past and their present results. For example, "If I'd cooked dinner earlier, (I didn't cook the dinner earlier) we would be eating now (but we aren't,) or, "They'd be happy (they aren't happy) if I'd bought them that toy (I didn't buy it.)

Two things to note about these conditional tenses are that:

1. We can invert the clauses, so "If I got lost in this jungle, I'd never find my way home," can become, "I'd never find my way home if I got lost in this jungle." We just need to omit the comma when doing this.

2. Traditionally, "If I were..." has been considered better English than, "If I was..." Nowadays, however, the latter is becoming much more common in spoken English and can't really be considered "wrong." I would mention this to your students and stress that, "If I were..." is still the correct form in written English, especially formal written English.

Hypothesizing

Using conditional sentences is not the only way we can talk about imagined events and actions. Let's look at four other common structures.

wish + past simple

Examples: "I wish (wish) you were happier (past simple)" or "I wish (wish) she drove better (past simple.)"

We use this structure when we want to talk about how we want things to be different in the present. So, for example, "I wish I were a football player" (I'm not a football player, but I want to be) or "I wish you loved me" (You, unfortunately, do not love me, but I want you to.)

if only + past simple

Examples: "If only (if only) you could sing (past simple) " or "If only (if only) it wasn't so hot (past simple.)"

And we use this one in the same way as the structure above, that is, to express how we wish things were different in the present. So, for example, "If only I were rich!" (I am, unfortunately, not rich, but I wish I were) or "If only I ate less" (I eat too much but wish I didn't.)

If only+ past perfect

Examples: "If only (if only) you hadn't burnt (past perfect) the dinner" or "If only (if only) you had asked (past perfect) me yesterday!"

We use this structure to talk about past events and actions and how we wish they had / hadn't occurred. For example, "If I only I hadn't left the door open" (I did leave the door open and wish I hadn't) or "If only you had asked me earlier" (You asked me too late.)

I wish + past perfect

Examples: "I wish (I wish) I had bought (past perfect) a Mercedes" or "I wish (I wish) they had done (past perfect) their homework."

We use this structure in the same way as the one above. So, for example, "I wish I had learned to swim" (I didn't learn to swim, but I want to have learned to swim) or "I wish my wife hadn't lost her wedding ring" (my wife lost her wedding ring and I want her not to have done so.)

Tag questions

Tag questions are a type of question that we use when we wish to check something we believe to be true or to check something we are unsure about. They are made up of a normal affirmative or negative sentence plus a short tag on the end. This type of question form is very common in spoken English and adds variety and color to our speech.

Structure for affirmative sentence: affirmative sentence + tag (Tag is made up of: negative auxiliary or modal verb + pronoun.)

Structure for negative sentence: negative sentence + tag (Tag is made up of positive auxiliary or modal verb + pronoun.

Please note that the auxiliary verb of the tag must always agree in tense and person.

Examples: "You're hungry, (affirmative sentence) aren't you (negative auxiliary verb + pronoun)?" or "You haven't been swimming, (negative sentence) have you (positive auxiliary verb + pronoun)?"

Let's look at forming tag questions in a bit more detail by running through some examples with different tense and forms.

"He is hot": Just take the auxiliary "be," change it into a negative and add the pronoun to form the tag question, "He's hot, isn't he?"

"They were angry": In the same manner, take the auxiliary verb "be," change it into a negative and add the pronoun to form the tag question, "They were angry, weren't they?"

"She's been to London": This one is slightly different as it contains the auxiliary verb, "have," but it's just as easy to form. Simply take the auxiliary, "have," change it into a negative and add the pronoun to form the tag question, "She's been to London, hasn't she?"

"That must be them": This ones got a modal in it, so we use that in its negative form and add the pronoun to form the tag question, "That must be them, mustn't it?"

Let's try one in the negative:

"He hadn't seen me": Ok, simply take the auxiliary have, make it positive and add the pronoun to form the tag question, "He hadn't seen me, had he?"

There are only a few things that you may need to stress to your students: Firstly, if a sentence contains no auxiliary verb, then simply use the correct form and tense of the verb, "do" e.g. "he likes coffee" becomes, "he likes coffee, doesn't he?" or "They went home" becomes, "They went home, didn't they?"; secondly, sentences that start "I am," take the tag, "aren't I," not "amn't!" So, "I'm tall, aren't I," for example; and finally, we rarely use "May" in tag questions. When we do, it is used to express probability and we, a little bizarrely, use the tag, "might." So, "We may eat later, mightn't we?" or "She may love him, mightn't she?"

Intonation

As mentioned above, we use tag questions for two
reasons: to check something we believe to be true; and to
check something we are unsure about. Our pronunciation
differs depending on which of these two reasons we are
using the tag question for. If we believe something to be
true and merely wish to verify it, then our intonation on
the tag part of the sentence stays level or falls; In a sense
it isn't really a question –we are just checking. However,
if we are unsure about something, then our intonation on
the tag part of the sentence rises. Try it, and you'll see
how you naturally raise your intonation if you are unsure
and keep it level or drop it on things you are surer about.

Comparative adjectives

Structure: Comparative adjective + than

Examples: "bigger (comparative adj) than (than,)" "more intelligent (comparative adj) than (than,)" "happier (comparative adj) than (than)" or "better (comparative adj) than (than.)"

We use comparative adjectives to say how two nouns, or things, differ. For example, "The city is nosier than the country."

Forming regular comparative adjectives:

This is relatively simple. For adjectives of one syllable, we simply add "er" to the adjective and double the final consonant if the adjective ends with vowel + consonant + vowel. For example, "I'm younger than you" or, "It is hotter here than in Denmark."

For adjectives of two or more syllables, except those that end in "y," we use: more + adjective + than. For example, "History is more interesting than geography" or, "Lions are more dangerous than mice."

For adjectives ending in "y" we simply change the "y" to "ier." For example, "I'm happier than I used to be," or, "Canadians are funnier than Americans."

Irregular comparative adjectives

The most common irregular comparative adjectives are: "good," which becomes, "better"; "bad," which becomes, "worse"; "well (healthy)," which becomes, "better"; and, "far," which becomes, "farther / further."

Superlative adjectives

Structure: superlative adjective!

Examples: "the biggest," "the most complicated," "the silliest" or, "the worst."

We use superlative adjectives to say which, of a group of things, has the most extreme quality. For example, we could say, "The Inland Taipan is the most venomous snake in the world (I think!)"

Forming superlative adjectives:

As with comparative adjectives, this is relatively simple. For one syllable adjectives, except those that end in "y," we simply use, "the" + adjective + "est" and double the final consonant if the adjective ends with vowel + consonant + vowel. For example, "The giraffe is the tallest mammal" or, "James is the fattest of my friends."

For adjectives of two or more syllables, except those that end in "y," we use, "the" + "most" + adj. For example, "She is the most beautiful woman I've ever seen" or, "the most nutritious thing I have in the house is pizza."

For adjectives ending in "y" we simply change the, "y" to, "iest." For example, "She's the funniest person here" or, "It's the foggiest day in a while."

Irregular superlative adjectives

The most common irregular superlative adjectives are: "good," which becomes, "the best"; "bad," which becomes, "the worst"; "well (healthy)," which becomes, "the best"; and, "far" which becomes, "farthest / furthest."

Phrases and clauses

Phrases

A phrase is a collection of words that work together to function as a part or element of a sentence, for example, a noun, an adjective or adverb etc. They never contain a subject that does a verb. So, remember, if you see a subject doing a verb, it's not a phrase!

Examples: "A big black dog bit me," "Throwing a baseball properly takes time and practice," or "I put the car in the garage."

So to find the phrases in the examples above, simply look for a collection of words that function as a single unit but do not contain a subject doing a verb. As you can probably discern, in the above examples the phrases are: "A big black dog." This phrase is functioning as a noun, so we call it, a noun phrase; "Throwing a baseball properly." This phrase is functioning as a gerund, so we call it a gerund (ive) phrase; and, "in the garage." This phrase is functioning as a preposition, so we call it, yes that's right! a prepositional phrase.

So, put very simply, phrases are simply parts of a sentence that don't contain subjects doing verbs! It's that simple.

Clauses

Examples: "When he opened the beer, it sprayed everywhere!" "After we had watched the movie, we went home" "They ate the pizza even though they didn't like anchovies" or "He likes coffee, and he likes tea."

As I emphasized, perhaps over-emphasized above, phrases don't contain subjects doing verbs. Clauses, on the other hand, do. There are two types of clauses: independent clauses and dependent (or subordinating) clauses.

Independent clauses

Independent clauses contain both a subject and a verb and can stand alone as a sentence. So for example in the sentence, "After we had watched the movie, we went home," "we went home." is an independent clause. It has the necessary: a subject and a verb, and can stand alone just by capitalizing the first word, "we": "We went home." In the sentence, "When he opened the beer, it sprayed everywhere," the second clause, "it sprayed everywhere," has a subject and a verb and all we need to do is to capitalize the "i" to change it into a sentence: "It sprayed everywhere."

An independent clause can be attached to a dependent clause using a subordinating conjunction (see below) or to another independent clause using a coordinating conjunction. The coordinating conjunctions are: "and," "but," "for," "yet," "so," "or" and "nor." For example, "He likes coffee, and he likes tea," "we don't go running everyday, but we do go on the weekend" or "They caught a fish, so they ate it for their dinner."

Dependent / subordinate clauses

A dependent, or subordinate, clause again contains a subject and a verb but is introduced by a subordinate conjunction and cannot stand alone as a sentence. Subordinate, or subordinating, conjunctions include: "after," "since," "when," "as," "if," "though," "where," "when," "before," "because," "after," "even though," "although" and "that."

So, in the sentence, "After we had watched the movie, we went home," the first clause contains a subject, a verb and the subordinating conjunction "after." It cannot stand alone as a sentence no matter what we do with the punctuation. Hence, it is a dependent clause. In the sentence, "They ate the pizza even though they didn't like anchovies," we can see that the clause, "even though they didn't like anchovies" contains the subordinating conjunction, "even though," a subject and a verb. Hence, it is a dependent clause and cannot stand alone as a sentence. A dependent clause must always be attached to an independent clause.

The Infinitive of purpose

Structure: to + base form of the verb

Examples: "We went to the park to (to) play (base form
of the verb,)" I went to the Post Office to (to) send (base
form of the verb) a letter" or, "They came to (to) see
(base form of the verb) how I was."

This is an extremely common structure that we would
teach during almost all elementary level courses. We use
it to express purpose; to say why we do something. For
example, "I went home." Why did I go home? "To make
dinner." So, "I went home to make dinner." Or, "She got
into the car." Why did she get into the car? "To drive to
work." So, "She got into the car to drive to work."

More formally, we can replace, "to" with, "in order to."
For example, "She studied hard to / in order to get into a
good college" or, "They went out to / in order to get some
fresh air."

Verb patterns

When we use more than one verb in a sentence, things can sometimes get just a little complicated. There are several accepted patterns that we use when we insert more than one verb. Here are some of the most common.

Verb + infinitive (with to)

Examples: "I want (verb) to go (infinitive with to) now" or "I promised (verb) to help (infinitive with to) him later."

This is one of our most common verb patterns and is fairly simple for students to grasp. The problem is that not all verbs can be followed by "to + infinitive." Unfortunately there is no rule for which verbs we can or can't use so students must simple learn them. Exposure to English in all its forms will greatly aid this. Some of the most common verbs that can be followed with "to + infinitive" are: "want," "learn," "hope," "choose," "help," "expect," "forget," "agree," "learn," "intend," "promise," "prepare" and "arrange."

Verb + verb+ing

Examples: "I detest (verb) cleaning (verb+ing)" or "I finish (verb) working (verb+ing) at 7:00pm."

Again, a very common pattern, but with the same problems for students; there are no rules for which verbs can be followed by verb+ing. Some of the most common that can be followed by verb+ing include: "enjoy," "adore," "can't," "stand," "admit," "consider," "advise," "avoid," "consider," "dislike," "quit," "practice," "delay," "keep," and "don't mind."

Note: There are some verbs that can be followed by either the infinitive or the ing form with little or no change of meaning: some of the most common of these verbs are: "start," "love," "attempt," "begin," "like," "hate," "begin," "prefer" and "continue." There are also, conversely, verbs that change the meaning of a sentence depending on whether they are followed by the infinitive or ing form. Some of the most common of these are: "come," "forget," "stop," "try" and "remember."

Verb + object + to + infinitive

Examples: "I asked (verb) him (object) to (to) go (infinitive)" or "We expected (verb) it (object) to (to) work (infinitive.)"

Some of the most common verbs used in this way are: "advise," "allow," "ask," "expect," "encourage," "get," "invite," "leave," "prefer," "teach," "tell" and "want."

Verb +object+ infinitive (without to)

Examples: "We made (verb) him (object) eat (infinitive)" or "We'll help (verb) him (object) improve (infinitive) his Spanish."

There aren't many verbs we use in this fashion, but the ones that we do are quite common. These verbs are: "make," "let" and "help."

As an aside, not all languages differentiate between the words, "make" and "let." The differences are that, "make" means "force to do" whereas "let" means "allow to do."

Verb + object + past participle

Examples: "I'm going to have (verb) my hair (object) cut (past participle)" or "I got (verb) my car (object) washed (past participle.)"

This is pattern is used most commonly with the verbs I used above for examples: "have" and "get." It's a lovely little structure and is used when somebody performs an action for somebody else. Other examples include: "I got my pants taken up" or "I am having my house repainted."

Reported speech

Examples: "He said he liked fish," "They told me they were coming later" or "I asked him if he was happy."

We use reported speech to report to others what has been said. For example, "John said that he had opened the door." In direct speech this would be, "I opened the door." Essentially when you report speech, you move back a tense, so the present simple tense becomes the past simple tense, the present continuous tense becomes the past continuous the past simple tense becomes the past perfect tense, and so on. Let's look at some examples:

Reported Statements

Direct statement: "I love donuts" (present simple tense.)

Becomes,

Reported statement: "She /he said (that) she loved donuts" (past simple tense.)

You may also have to change the pronoun:

Direct speech: "My mum saw a ghost!" (past simple tense.)

Becomes,

Reported statement: "She/ he said that (that) his/her mum

had seen a ghost!" (past perfect tense.)

So, in complete:

The present simple becomes the past simple.

The present continuous becomes the past continuous.

The present perfect tense becomes the past perfect.

The present perfect continuous becomes the past perfect continuous.

The past simple becomes the past perfect.

The past simple continuous becomes the past perfect continuous.

The past perfect tense and past perfect continuous don't change.

And,

"Will" becomes "would."

"Can" becomes "could."

Reported questions

Examples: "Tony asked if we were going to come over for dinner later," "He asked me where the pens were," or "She wanted to know whether you had her coat."

Reported questions aren't much trickier but do require you to do several things:

1. Insert words such as, "They asked" or "She wanted to know" at the start of the reported question.

2. Change the question into its affirmative form if necessary: so, subject + verb.

3. Change the tense of course, just as we would in reported statements.

4. Omit any example of the auxiliary verb "do." (Only when it is used as an auxiliary verb though. Not as "to do.")

5. Insert "if" /"whether" for yes / no questions.

6. Change the pronoun if necessary.

7. Omit question marks.

Let's look at some examples of direct questions and how we can change the structure to reported questions:

Direct question: "How are you?"

So simply change the tense of the question to the past simple, change the word order to a normal affirmative sentence, that is, subject + verb, and change the pronoun from "you" to "I." It becomes:

Reported question: "She / he asked me how I was."

Another one:

Direct question: "Where did you eat yesterday?"
So, change the tense of the question to the past perfect. The word order is already affirmative (subject + verb) so we can leave that, but we do need to omit the "do." Change the pronoun and it becomes.

Reported question: "He / she asked me where I'd eaten yesterday."

One more:

Direct question: "Do you want a sandwich?"

So: change the tense to the past simple; change the pronoun; the word order is affirmative, so leave that; omit the auxiliary "do"; and finally, insert "if" or "whether" because this is a yes / no question. So it becomes:

Reported question: "He / she asked me if I wanted a sandwich."

Relative clauses

Structure: Relative pronoun + clause

Examples: "The coat which (relative pronoun) I wore yesterday (clause) is in the cupboard" or, "We ate the cake that (relative pronoun) Steven had baked (clause)."

We use relative clauses to give more information about a noun or noun phrase. In a sense they form the same function as an adjective, hence their other names, adjective or adjectival clauses. We introduce relative clauses with a relative pronoun which can function as the object or subject of the clause.

The relative pronouns

The relative pronouns are: "who," for people and as a subject or object pronoun; "which," for things and animals and as a subject or object pronoun; "whose," for possession for people, animals and things; "whom," for people and as an object pronoun; "where" for places and as a object pronoun; "that" for people, animals and things, as a subject or object pronoun, but only in defining relative clauses (more on these later.)

Please note that strictly speaking, "where" is a relative adverb, but it serves the same purpose as a relative pronoun and carries the meaning of, "in which."

Subject pronoun relative clauses

Structure: Relative pronoun + verb

Example: "The dog which (relative pronoun) is (verb) eating the bone is mine" or, "That man who (relative pronoun) is (verb) cleaning his car is my brother."

Object pronoun relative clauses

Structure: Relative pronoun + noun / pronoun + verb

Examples: "A popular movie that (relative pronoun) I (pronoun) have (verb) seen is The Godfather" or, "I read the book that (relative pronoun) Mike (noun) had (verb) left at my house."

Defining relative clauses

Examples: "That boy who is climbing the tree is my son" or "Can I try on those shoes that have green soles."

Defining relative clauses contain information that is vital to the meaning of the sentence. Hence, we cannot omit this clause. So, for the examples above, imagine several children playing in a park. I might say, "That boy who is climbing the tree is my son." Without the information, "who is climbing the tree" the listener would not know which boy I was referring to; or, imagine shopping in a shoe store. You might ask the assistant, "Can I try on those shoes that have green soles ?" Without the information, "that have green soles" the assistant would not know which shoes you were referring to.

Non-defining relative clauses

Examples: "The Blue whale, which feeds on krill, is the largest mammal in the world" or "Man first landed on the moon in 1969, which was the same year Charles de Gaulle stepped down as president of France."

Non-defining relative clauses contain information that is not vital to the meaning of the sentence. These clauses can be omitted without changing the meaning of the sentence and are enclosed in commas. For example, "The Blue whale, which feeds on krill, is the largest mammal in the world." We don't need to include the information, "which feed on krill" for the sentence to make sense and we could happily omit it. Or, "Man first landed on the moon in 1969, which was the same year Charles de Gaulle stepped down as president of France." Again, we can clearly omit, "which was the same year…" without changing the meaning of the sentence.

Phrasal verbs

Phrasal verbs are very common in everyday English speech and are often very idiomatic. They are made up of a verb and a particle(s) (Very simply, a particle is a preposition that is not acting in the manner of a preposition.) Phrasal verbs may be transitive or intransitive, and transitive phrasal verbs may be separable or inseparable. Let's examine the four major kinds of phrasal verbs in more detail:

verb + particle (intransitive)

Examples: "I got (verb) up (particle) at 6:00 o'clock" or "My car broke (verb) down (particle) yesterday."

Intransitive verbs, or in this case intransitive phrasal verbs, DO NOT take an object. Other examples of this kind of phrasal verb include: "break in," "come over," "doze off," "get along," "speak up," "eat out" and "end up."

verb + particle (transitive and separable)

Examples: "Pick (verb) up (particle) the pen" or "I turned (verb) up (particle) the TV."

Transitive phrasal verbs DO take an object, as in the examples above: "pen" and "TV." And, as this kind of verb is separable the object can come between the verb and its particle. So, "Pick the pen up" or "I turned the TV up." If the object is a pronoun it MUST come between the verb and its object. For example, "I'll pick you up at 7:00" not "I'll pick up you at seven." Other examples of this kind of phrasal verb include: "send back," "take off," "take apart," "fill up," "take down," and "wash up."

verb + particle (transitive and inseparable)

Examples: "I get (verb) off (particle) the bus at Mayfair" or "It took me a long time to get (verb) over (particle) my illness."

So, as these kinds of phrasal verbs are inseparable we CANNOT put the object between the verb and particle. "I get the bus off" or "I get my illness over," for example, are obviously incorrect English. Other examples of this kind of phrasal verb include: "get to," "give out," "keep off," "pick on" and "keep on."

verb + particle + particle (transitive and inseparable)

Examples: "I have to put (verb) up (particle) with (particle) a lot of noise at work" or "I'm happy when I look (verb) back (particle) on (particle) my childhood."

This final phrasal verb structure is usually heavily idiomatic and so is often the hardest for students to remember. Other examples of this kind of phrasal verb include: "look in on," "look up to," "put down to," "brush up on" and "look down on."

Gerunds

Structure: Verb+ing

Examples: "Running (verb+ing) is good for you health," "I love eating(verb+ing,)" "Reading (verb+ing) is an excellent way to spend your time," "Renovating (verb+ing) old furniture can be a satisfying hobby" or "The coca cola is only for drinking (verb+ing) if you get really tired!"

Gerunds are verb+ing forms that function, primarily, as the subject or object of a sentence. In addition, we can use them as the compliment to a preposition. Let's look at some gerunds in the wild so to speak.

Gerund used as subject

Examples: "Smoking is bad for you" or "Relaxing can get boring after a while."

Nothing too complex here, the gerund is simply functioning as a noun would.

Gerund used as direct object

Example: "I like swimming" or "We hate working."

Again, nothing too complex here. Again, the gerund simply functions as a noun would but this time as an object. Let's move along.

Gerund phrase used as a subject

Examples: "Drinking too much in the evening gives you a hangover "or "Waiting around all day makes me tired."

Just a little more complex, we're using a gerund phrase. (A gerund phrase is simply a group of words, including a gerund, but no verb, that function as a noun, and in this case as the subject of the sentence.) So, in the first sentence, "Drinking too much in the evening" is the subject phrase and in the second sentence, "Waiting around all day" is the subject phrase.

Gerund phrase used as object

Examples: "I love sitting in the sun" or "She can't stand being alone."

So here, we are again using a gerund phrase, but as the object. In the first sentence, "sitting in the sun" is the object phrase and in the second, "being alone" is the object phrase. (To find your object or object phrase, just ask yourself "what?" i.e. "What does she/ he love?" Answer: "Sitting in the sun" or "What can't she stand? Answer: "being alone."

Gerund phrase used as preposition compliment

Note: We are using, "Compliment" to mean something along the lines of, "Gives more information about," in this case the preposition.

Examples: "On seeing the ghost, I ran!" "I might buy a new chair for relaxing in the evening" or "By eating well you live longer."

This structure is somewhat uncommon in most constructions but relatively common when using for + gerund phrase. For example, "I bought it for getting to work" or "It's not for playing with!"

Grammatical differences between American and British English

Most people are familiar with vocabulary differences between American and British English e.g. hood / bonnet, pants / trousers, soccer / football etc. There are also, however, a couple of important grammatical differences:

Past simple vs. present perfect

In American English there is a tendency to utilize the past simple tense for past actions with present results, whereas in British English people would tend to use the present perfect tense. For example, in American English, "I ate already" would indicate that I have eaten and that I am now full (probably,) whereas native British English speakers would probably say, "I have eaten already." Or, in American English, "I saw that movie, it was great" but, in British English, "I've seen that movie. It was great."

Got / gotten

In American English the past participle of the verb "Get" is "Gotten" whereas in British English it's, "Got." So American English speakers might say, "Have you gotten paid yet?" whereas British English speakers would say, "Have you got paid yet?" Or, in American English, "My brother has gotten better at Spanish" but, in British English, "My brother has got better at Spanish."

Other grammatical differences are negligible and really only a matter of academic interest rather that having any practical importance in the classroom. I would recommend you teach whichever forms you are more familiar with and just make your students aware of any differences rather than stressing them.

102 ESL Games and Activities for New and Prospective Teachers (extract)

Introduction

Students need to practice the various grammatical structure in-class to internalize them and thus be able to produce them outside of class in real-life situations. You will find the following activities extracted from the book 102 ESL Games and Activities for New and Prospective Teachers an excellent way to get your students practicing various grammatical structures in a fun, interactive manner.

Extract

A Valentine's story

Language / Skill practiced: Past simple

Time: 30 mins

Language level: Elementary to intermediate

Arrange the class, on chairs, into a circle and give each student a sheet of paper. Explain to the class that they are going to write a love or Valentine's story and that they must write full sentence answers to your questions. Ask your first question, "What was his name?" Each student writes the answer at the top of her piece of paper and then folds the paper back so that the sentence is hidden. They then pass their piece of paper to the student on their left and answer your next question, "What was her name?" before folding back the paper once more and again passing it to the person on their left. Continue in this way for about ten questions, asking questions such as, "What did he say to her?" "Where did they go?" "Where did they have their first kiss?" etc. When you have finished asking questions, ask the students to read their stories and, if you choose, correct any errors.

The truth or a dirty lie?

Language / Skill practiced: Various / Fluency skills

Time: 30 mins

Language level: Pre–intermediate to advanced

Ask students write down, on a sheet of paper, three sentences about themselves, two of which are true and one a lie. For example, "I lived in Italy for two years when I was younger," "I can juggle" and "I drink 10 cups of coffee a day." Put students into pairs and ask them to swap their pieces of paper. Both students must pretend that all the sentences they wrote are true. Students take turns to question their partner to try and determine which is a lie.

S1 (reading S2's first sentence): I lived in Italy for two years when I was younger. Hmm. Why were you in Italy?

S2: My Dad had a job there.

S1: What did he do?

S2: Um, um a doctor, he was a doctor!

S1: Really? Are there a lot of Japanese doctors working in Italy?

S2: Um, yes. I think so.

S1: Hmmm. Ok, next sentence

When each student has had a chance to question his partner about her sentences, ask them to make a guess as to which sentence of their partner's is a lie.

Frequency predictions

Language / Skill practiced: Present simple / Adverbs and expressions of frequency

Time: 15 mins

Language level: Elementary to pre - intermediate

Prepare sets of cards on which you have written adverbs and expressions of frequency, such as "sometimes," "often," "once a week" and so on. Divide the class into pairs and give each pair a set of cards face down. Students take it in turns to pick a card from the pack and ask their partner a question in order to elicit the word on the card. For example:

S1 (Picks card that says always): How often do you brush your teeth in the morning.

S2: Usually.

S1: Really! Ok, um. How often do you drink beer in the evening?

S2: Always. I always drink beer.

S1: Great, you got it. Your turn.

I've never felt the need to instigate a scoring system with this activity.

About the Author

Miles Jaworski has been an English language teacher for 25 years and has worked in countries as diverse as China, Vietnam, Ecuador and the United States of America.

Other books by this author

102 ESL Games and Activities for New and Prospective Teachers

102 ESL Games and Activities for Kids

English Grammar Exercises: A Complete Guide to English Tenses for ESL Students

CPSIA information can be obtained at www.ICGtesting.com
Printed in the USA
LVOW04s1742051015

456971LV00022B/987/P